the book of escapes

THE BOOK OF ESCAPES

by Tom Mason and Dan Danko
with John Railing and Danny Orleans, Professional Magicians

Scholastic Inc.

New York • Toronto • London • Auckland • Sydney
Mexico City • New Delhi • Hong Kong • Buenos Aires

ISBN 0-439-32705-9

Copyright © 2001 by Scholastic Inc.

Design by Mark Neston
Illustrations by Daniel Aycock

12 11 10 9 8 7 6 5 4 3 2 1   1 2 3 4 5 6/0

Printed in the U.S.A.

First Scholastic printing, January 2002

tABLe of CoNtENts

the great escape artist

Escape.

If there's one guy who knew everything about escaping, it was Harry Houdini (1874-1926). He'd wear a straight jacket, get put inside a box, have chains wrapped around the box, and then the box would get thrown into water. You know what Houdini'd do next?

If you said "drown," you'd be wrong. But that's what the audience thought. Instead, he escaped! And he did it over and over again. He escaped from everything from simple handcuffs to jail cells to giant steel crates.

And Houdini never stopped. For publicity, he once took a trip to England and issued a challenge to Scotland Yard, which had a reputation as the world's greatest police force in the early twentieth century.

Houdini challenged them to lock him up. They probably thought Houdini was just a crazy tourist, but they accepted his offer. They handcuffed his hands together and put him in their best jail.

And Houdini escaped.

That daring trick made him famous all over the world. But what's that got to do with you and Magic University?

Everything.

This month at Magic U., you're going to learn many of Houdini's best secrets—not all of them, of course, but enough to get you started! You'll be able to escape from rope ties and thumb ties, chains and locks and even a chair. As you go through your "At-Home Escapes," you'll even find out how to help others —specifically a ring, a Life Saver and a Cheerio— escape from string. Hey, apprentice magicians have got to start somewhere!

Unlike many other tricks here at Magic U., escapes require someone to help you practice. Houdini was a master escape artist, but even he couldn't tie himself up! If there are secrets to be revealed (aren't there always?), be sure to choose someone who won't give them away. Secrecy is the first rule of good magic!

As you are mastering your "Escapes," take a look at some of the different principles involved in making these tricks work. Some tricks work because of *topology*; that is, they depend on what happens when a geometric shape—for example, the circle formed by a loop of rope—is changed or altered in some way (like by stretching).

Other tricks work because you're a bit sneaky: For example, you secretly break something and pretend that you haven't. Or you make a move that's so quick that the audience can't see what really happened.

So practice, practice, and then practice some more. Who knows, you might someday be ready to issue a challenge to Scotland Yard of your own, just like master "escapologist" Harry Houdini!

—Tom Mason and Dan Danko

kNot to WORRy!

E scaping is all about getting out of knotty situations. But before you get out of 'em, you have to get into 'em. And that means learning to tie knots! So here are the how-tos for three knots that you'll have to pick up before you can do the tricks.

overHand kNot

This is the first knot you probably ever learned. You use it to tie your sneakers.

STEP 1: Hold one end of a string or rope in your left hand and the other end in your right hand.

STEP 2: Cross the two ends, forming a loop.

STEP 3: Put one end of the string or rope through the loop.

STEP 4: Pull both ends of the string or rope to tighten the knot.

square kNot

STEP 1: Make a loose **overhand knot**, following steps 1 through 4 above for that knot. The knot should be loose enough that you can still see a loop when you're done.

STEP 2: Make another overhand knot by again following steps 1 through 4 for the **overhand knot** above. But if you created the loop for the first knot by putting the left end of the string or rope over the right end of the string or rope, then tie the second knot by putting the right end over the left end. If your first knot was tied by putting the right end over the left end, then make the second knot by putting the left end over the right end.

STEP 3: Pull the ends of the string or rope away from each other. This will make the top overhand knot tighten against the lower overhand knot, making a square knot.

sLip kNot

STEP 1: Make a big loop at one end of a piece of string or rope. Make sure that you leave a couple of inches free at the short end of the string or rope dangling from the loop.

STEP 2: Fold the short end of the string or rope dangling free from the loop in half, as if you were about to make a second loop.

STEP 3: Push this folded piece through the loop, and tighten the long end of string or rope dangling from the loop. And there's your slip knot!

STEP 4: If you want to get rid of the knot, pull the ends of the string or rope on either side of the loop, and the knot will untie itself.

the tricks

THE STRING PULL #1

assignment: Remove a ball tied between two strings!

the escaping ball

How can a ball escape from two pieces of string? When the two pieces of string aren't really tied together, that's how! The strings are just looped together inside the ball and pull apart very easily.

magic must-haves: Magic trunk

from your escapes kit: One red ball, two strings, plastic box

backstage

Remember those tricks where you didn't have to do any preparation? Ha! This isn't one of them.

STEP 1: Fold each string in half.

STEP 2: Insert the loop of one string (let's call it string A) into the other (let's call it string B).

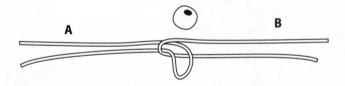

STEP 3: Thread the two ends of string B into the hole in the ball.

STEP 4: Carefully push the ball along folded string B until the overlapping loops go into the hole and are hidden from view.

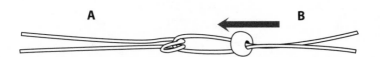

STEP 5: The ball should now look like it has two strings threaded through it.

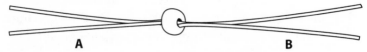

STEP 6: Put the plastic box on the magic trunk.

STEP 7: There is no step 7! Your work here is done!

sHOW time!

"Ladies and gentlemen, I know this looks like a little plastic ball."

STEP 1: Hold up the ball with the ropes dangling out of it. Be careful that none of the strings fall out! If the ball slips out of your hand, kick it out of the room and yell, **"Goal!"** Then move on to the next trick.

"But let's pretend that this is Harry Houdini, the famous escape artist. And he's tied himself up again for another great escape. Who wants me to make it more difficult for Houdini?"

STEP 2: After a show of hands, put the ball into the plastic box. Adjust the strings so that they stick out through the side holes.

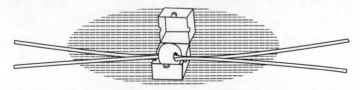

"The votes are in. Let's say good-bye to Mr. Houdini."

STEP 3: Close the box and set it on your magic trunk. Now study the box for a second and act like you're thinking.

"I don't know. It still looks pretty easy to me. Who wants me to make it even tougher for the master escape artist?"

STEP 4: After a show of hands, take one end of string from each side and gently tie a simple overhand knot on top of the closed box. (If you don't know what an overhand knot is, stay cool—just check out page 3).

"All right. That looks pretty tough."

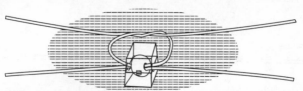

STEP 5: Hold on to the two ends of both strings—keeping the strings straight. Get ready to pull the strings in opposite directions—away from the box—at the same time. That way the box won't jump around when you pull the strings.

"Everybody count to three with me. One, two..."

STEP 6: Pull the strings in the opposite direction at the same time. The strings will release themselves from the ball and the box.

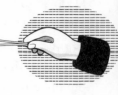

"...three!"

STEP 7: Hold up the strings to the audience.

"Guess I'll have to make it even harder for Houdini next time."

NOW TRY it THIS WAY!

If you're feeling really confident, don't do this trick on the magic trunk. Get a volunteer from the audience to hold the box in his closed hands. Then tie the knot over the back of the volunteer's hand and pull the strings.

OR TRY it THIS WAY!

Before tying the overhand knot, ask a volunteer to put her index finger on top of the box. Now tie the knot over her finger. This makes it even more amazing—and easier to do. The volunteer's finger will hold the box still and make a magical "escape" from the knot when you pull the strings apart!

extra credit: Get your volunteer to hold one or both ends of the strings while you hold the box in your hand or with one finger on the magic trunk. When they pull, they do the magic, but you get the credit. Sounds like a good deal to me! (Just make sure they don't pull too soon or your secret could be revealed.)

homework: Timing is everything here. After you've stuffed the strings inside the ball, practice pulling them out at the same time. It's gotta look smooth, and you've gotta do it just right.

A THING FOR STRING

The principle on which this trick (and many other rope and string tricks) is based was first published in 1584 in the first magic book ever: Reginald Scot's *The Discoverie of Witchcraft*. Back in those days, people were so frightened of sorcery and magic that they burned anyone who practiced it. Burning witches was quite popular in the 1400s and 1500s. Scot found this inhumane treatment revolting and used his book to reveal many conjuring tricks, so that he could demonstrate that people who seemed to be sorcerers were really just ordinary people doing ordinary things that only looked supernatural. This particular string trick was very popular in the 1800s, when it was called My Grandmother's Necklace. In that version, several beads magically released themselves from their string.

assigNment: Remove three balls from two strings!

tHe tHree of BaLLs

The two cords are threaded in a special way through the center bead. When you tie two of the ends in an overhand knot, you prepare the beads to make their great escape.

from your escapes kit: Three red beads, two
strings, and a partridge in a pear tree. (Oops. Just kidding about the partridge. And the pear tree.)

Homemade magic: One handkerchief

> **Trick Tip:** This trick should follow **The String Pull** in your act. It's based on the same principle, but uses more balls.

Backstage

If you've already done The String Pull trick, you should have a pretty good idea of what comes next.

STEP 1: Take your two strings and fold each string in half.

STEP 2: Insert one loop into the other.

A   B

STEP 3: Thread the two ends of string B into the hole in the ball.

A   B

STEP 4: Carefully push the ball along folded string B until the overlapping loops go into the hole and are hidden from view.

STEP 5: Now thread the other two beads onto each side of string A and string B.

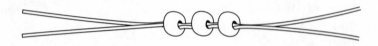

sноw time!
"I'm going to tell you a story about the old West."

STEP 1: Show the balls threaded on the two strings.

"Once upon a time, back when the West was really wild, there were three outlaw brothers, Joe, Jack, and Jim."

Trick Tip: Don't let the balls slide back and forth on the string too much, or the audience will see that the middle one is stuck in place.

STEP 2: Hold the ends of the strings in each hand, and shake the balls around a little. This proves to the audience that the balls are securely on the string!

"They were bank robbers, but they were also escape artists."

STEP 3: Take one string from each side of the balls and tie them together in a simple overhand knot on top of the balls. (Check out page 3 for that overhand knot.)

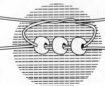

"One time, they got caught by the sheriff."

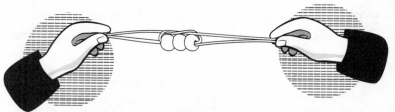

STEP 4: Pull the knot tight—but not too tight or the secret loops might fall out of the center ball.

"He tied them up with his best rope..."

STEP 5: Cover the balls with the handkerchief. Put your hands underneath the handkerchief.

"...and threw them into a dark, dark jail."

STEP 6: Look straight at the audience. When you make eye contact with them, they'll make eye contact with you and that'll keep them from paying too much attention to your hands!

"Then the sheriff went down to the saloon to celebrate his victory over the three brothers."

STEP 7: While your hands are underneath the handkerchief, pull on the ends of the strings and the loops will come

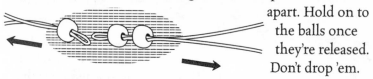

apart. Hold on to the balls once they're released. Don't drop 'em.

"But he forgot the first rule of good sheriffing—never leave three brothers alone in the same jail."

STEP 8: Pull the handkerchief away. The balls have magically escaped from the strings. Hold the balls out to the audience.

"Because it doesn't take them very long to escape."

HOMEWORK: You have to do a lot of work underneath the handkerchief without looking at your hands. Practice pulling the strings apart in front of a mirror so you can learn to do it without looking down at your hands!

HOUÔINI, jR.

assignment: Free yourself from chains!

Lock Luck

Just like rope tricks, this all depends on how you wrap the chain around your hands. You're not really chained as securely as the audience thinks you are—the lock just makes them believe it more!

from your escapes kit: The chain, padlock, and key

extras: A volunteer from the audience. (They don't have to know your secret, but they do have to know how to follow your instructions!)

Backstage

If you study the chain, you'll notice that it has two rings hooked into it. This will be important in the trick. If you like to count, count the number of links in the chain. It won't help you at all, but it'll keep you from bothering people (unless you count out loud).

Show time!

"Lots of people think escape artists use special gimmicks and gadgets to fool their audience. Not true. Check out this chain."

STEP 1: Hold up the chain and the lock to the audience.

"Notice the two rings in the chain and this lock."

STEP 2: Pass the chain around to the audience, but keep the lock.

"Take a look at this chain. Pull it, tug it, look it over. It's made of solid stuff and it's unbreakable."

STEP 3: Create a chain loop by inserting the end of the chain into the ring at the other end of the chain.

"I'm going to make this really tough on myself, just like Harry Houdini did when he escaped from chains."

"Now, I need a volunteer from the audience..."

STEP 4: Select your volunteer. Call her up from the audience.

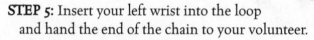

"Okay, come on up here!"

STEP 5: Insert your left wrist into the loop and hand the end of the chain to your volunteer.

"There, now you pull the loose end."

STEP 6: The loop should fit snugly around your left wrist. Here's a clue: The ring that the chain is pulled through should stay at the top of your wrist. This is the *key* to the whole escape! Say to your volunteer:

"Hey, whoa, I said pull the chain, not cut off my circulation!"

STEP 7: The loose end of the chain should now be hanging down on the inside of your left wrist. Now, put your hands together, interlocking your fingers and thumbs.

"Now, wrap the chain around my right wrist. I want it tight, but please, try not to tattoo me with the metal, okay?"

STEP 8: Have your volunteer pull the chain to your right, then up and over both your hands.

"See that second ring? Please put the loose end through it and pull the chain back up again."

15

STEP 9: After your volunteer has done this, have a little fun.

"OOOWWW! Take it easy. Good thing I didn't ask for your help with my special brick wall escape trick!"

Trick Tip: Pretending that the chain is really tight helps the audience believe that there's no way for you to escape. It's all about the acting!

STEP 10: Now have your volunteer pick up the lock and lock the loose end of the chain to part of the chain that's on top of your wrists.

"Okay, now take that lock and hook it onto the last link of the chain. Then lift the lock and hook it through the part of the chain that's wrapped around my wrists. Push the lock shut. Take your time. We want this done right and tight!"

STEP 11: You're done! The lock isn't gimmicked and neither is the chain. You can escape in less than three seconds. But you don't want the audience to see you do it, so start turning around in a circle.

"I can do this the easy way or the hard way."

STEP 12: Keep turning, and when your back is to the audience, unlock your fingers. Then lift your right wrist and rotate it toward your left wrist. You'll immediately feel the chain loosen.

"But you look like the kind of audience that wants to see me struggle."

Trick Tip: Before you do this trick for a live audience, you can practice the chain release by putting your hands under a handkerchief or under a table.

STEP 13: Continue to lift your right hand and the chain will drop.

"So I'll do it the hard way…and I hope that someone has the key, just in case."

STEP 14: By the time you turn back around to face the audience, you'll be out of the chain. And the best part? The chain is still locked. Pass the chain to the audience or just hold it out in front of them so they can see both chain and lock.

"There! That'll put the 'hoo' in Houdini."

HOMEWORK: The real trick is the wrapping of the chain. Practice it with a friend who can wrap you up. Your friend doesn't have to be the volunteer you call on from the audience later.

THE CHAIN GANG
This chain trick was created by P. T. Selbit in the early 1900s. If you remember your Magic U. history from *The Book of Illusions,* you'll also know him as the guy who invented the famous Sawing a Woman in Half trick.

---

it's in the Bag #4

assignment: Remove rings locked to a chain!

Lock it up!

You've guessed it already, haven't you? The rings aren't really locked into place! The chain is locked up tight, but it's really only wrapped around the rings, which makes it easy to unwind. Beauty!

magic must-haves: Magic trunk

from your escapes kit: Large ring, small ring, the chain, and the padlock

Homemade magic: A large paper bag—grocery store sized

> **Trick Tip:** The bag is where it all happens, but if you don't have a bag, you can use anything that's similar—a box, a trash can, even a backpack! Just make sure the audience can't see through it!

extras: One volunteer from the audience (someone who doesn't know the trick but can do what you say—don't you wish you had more friends like that?)

Backstage

Just make sure someone hasn't walked off with your grocery bag or thrown it away by accident!

show time!

"I'm going to tell you a story about Sheriff Carl and his trusty deputy, Yippie Kai Yay."

STEP 1: Hold up the two rings as you say the names.

"They were hot on the trail of a famous outlaw...a notorious bank robber named Ambush Pete."

STEP 2: Pick up the chain and fold it in half. Hold the two ends of the chain in your right hand.

"But as luck would have it, they were ambushed. That's right...ambushed by Ambush Pete."

STEP 3: Slip the ring over your left hand, and then grab the fold in the chain in your left hand as well. Let the ring fall off your hand, and slide to the center of the folded chain.

"Pete had big plans for his next bank robbery..."

STEP 4: Take the fold of the chain (that's in your left hand) and lift it over the top of the large ring. At the same time, thread the two ends of the chain through the loop you've formed with the folded chain.

"And he didn't want any interference from some crazy cowboy and a deputy called Yippie Kai Yay."

STEP 5: Pull the ends of the chain to create a knot around the large ring.

"So he used his special chain."

STEP 6: Thread the small ring through the two loose ends of the chain and let it go.

"And he tied up Sheriff Carl and Yippie Kai Yay..."

STEP 7: Now, it's the audience participation part everyone's been waiting for! Call up a volunteer and have her lock the two ends of the chain together.

"...locking the chain with his special lock."

STEP 8: Pick up the lock and hold it above your head. The chain will dangle while holding both the small and large rings.

"Then he did something that was even worse than that."

STEP 9: Ask your volunteer to hold the lock, so that the chain dangles down—just as you were holding it in the last step.

"Now, you hold this...and please don't let go!"

STEP 10: Open up the large paper grocery bag. Hold it open underneath the chain.

"Okay, now gently lower Sheriff Carl and Yippie into the bag...but keep holding on to the lock!"

STEP 11: Place the bag on the magic trunk. The bag should be high enough so that you can comfortably fit your hands inside, but the audience still can't see inside the bag!

"Ambush Pete lowered Sheriff Carl and Yippie into a dark, dark cave."

Reach into the bag with both hands. Raise the small ring just a little bit and move it out of the way.

"And Ambush Pete rode off to rob another bank."

STEP 12: Separate the two halves of the knot around the large ring and pull them to the sides of the ring. This sounds difficult, but it really isn't.

"It was cold in the cave. Dark, too."

STEP 13: Continue to push the knots in the chain to the bottom of the large ring.

"But that didn't stop Sheriff Carl, because his young deputy, Yippie Kai Yay, had more than just a funny name."

STEP 14: The large ring will slip off the chain followed by the small ring.

"He was a master escape artist."

STEP 15: Ask your volunteer to pull the chain out of the bag, as you remove both rings which have "escaped" from their shackles of bondage!

"Now, if only Yippie could remember where he left the horses!"

HOMEWORK: The bag is what makes your trick mysterious. So you can't do this trick until you can unhook the rings from the chain without looking! Practice using a mirror until you make this look easy.

CHAINS of LOVE #5

assignment: Escape after being chained to a friend!

shackled

This trick is a neat twist on what you did in #3: Houdini, Jr. Your quick escape from what seems to be a tightly locked chain appears even more miraculous here 'cause you're chained to someone else!

from your escapes kit: The chain, padlock, and key

homemade magic: A scarf, bandanna, or handkerchief

extras: You're going to need a friend from the audience. You'll be chaining yourselves together, so pick someone you really like and who isn't too stinky!

Trick Tip: This trick can either be done with someone who has secretly rehearsed with you and knows how to do the trick or with a volunteer who has no idea what's about to happen. Experiment both ways and decide which way works best for you. Just make sure your secret someone can *keep* a secret!

backstage

If you've already done other tricks with the chain, you've already noticed that it has two rings hooked into it. If you haven't, look closer! If you can see the two rings, you're ready to go!

show time!

"Did you know that there was an ancient marriage ceremony where the bride and groom were literally linked together?"

STEP 1: Show the chain to the audience. Let them hold it if you're feeling totally confident—don't worry, there's nothing for them to figure out!

"It was called The Chain of Marriage. See how the wedding rings are hooked onto the chain?"

STEP 2: Pick a person from the audience that you would like to "marry."

"Now, I need a volunteer spouse from the audience. Don't worry! This wedding comes with an easy divorce. I promise."

STEP 3: While your volunteer watches, create a chain loop by inserting the end of the chain into the ring at the opposite end.

"The chain is tough."

STEP 4: Form a loop in the chain.

"It's made of solid metal."

STEP 5: Insert your partner's left wrist through the loop. Stand on her left side. Pull on the loose end of the chain.

"And it's designed to bind a happy couple..."

STEP 6: Pull the chain tight. Be sure the ring that the chain is going through stays at the top of her wrist. This positioning is the key to the escape. The pull of the chain might be a bit tight, but now she'll know that this escape is "for real."

"...together for all eternity...sorry about that."

STEP 7: The loose end should now be hanging down on the inside of her wrist.

"Now, repeat after me. I, [her name], take [your name] to be my pretend spouse..."

STEP 8: Are you taller or shorter than your partner? Your answer depends on what to do next. Put your right arm over (if you're taller) or under (if you're shorter) her left arm so the inside of your forearms are touching. Interlock your fingers with hers.

"...at least until the end of this trick."

STEP 9: As she repeats the "vows," go ahead and do the wrapping. Let her help wherever it's needed. The end of the chain should be pulled up and to your right, then over the top of both of your wrists.

"Okay. My turn."

STEP 10: With your left hand, put the end of the chain through the other ring.

"I, [your name], take [her name] to be my pretend spouse..."

STEP 11: Pull the chain up and over your wrists again to your left. Have your partner use her right hand to lock the loose end to the body of the chain.

"...at least until the end of this trick. I now pronounce us pretend husband and pretend wife."

STEP 12: Can you see it yet? The chain and the lock are not gimmicked. Even so, you can still escape in less than three seconds—about the time it takes to gobble down an Oreo. But you really don't want the audience to see your escape.

Cover your hands with the scarf, bandanna, or handkerchief, or put your hands under a table out of sight of the audience.

"But not all marriages last forever."

STEP 13: As you say this, lift your right wrist and rotate it toward her left wrist. You'll immediately feel the chain loosen.

"And that's the great thing about this ancient ceremony."

STEP 14: Continue to lift and twist your right hand and the chain will drop.

"As quickly as we got married..."

STEP 15: By the time you've finished speaking, you should be out of the chain.

"...we can get divorced."

STEP 16: Hold the chain up to the audience. The chain is still locked!

"But don't worry. We can still be friends!"

Trick Tip: Once you've practiced this a lot and feel really comfortable with it, you can add in "The Wedding Dance." Just start dancing around your partner, freeing yourself whenever your wrists can't be seen by the audience.

HOMEWORK: You'll want to practice the wrapping of the chains with a friend—someone you can trust with the secret. But you'll also want to practice the escape without looking at your hands! Try it in front of a mirror a few times until you can do it easily!

assignment: Remove a ring from a double-knotted rope!

the new twist

When you twist the rope twice, it looks like you're really doubling up the knot. But you're not! By twisting just the right way, your second twist cancels out your first one, freeing the ring without ever tying it up!

from your escapes kit: The large metal ring, the rope

extras: You're going to need a volunteer to help you with the tying...or is it really untying?

backstage

Is there anything easier than a magic trick that requires no preparation? You've probably got time to hit the fridge and down some juice.

show time!

"Who here is good with knots?"

STEP 1: Lots of people think they're good with knots, and lots of hands will shoot up. Look around the room carefully like you're giving it a lot of thought, then make your selection. There's no real reason for the "thinking," it's just kind of fun!

"I'm going to need some help. But don't worry, you won't get hurt."

STEP 2: Thread the ring through the rope. Keep one end of the rope in your left hand and give the other end to your volunteer.

"Well, at least I don't think you'll get hurt."

VOLUNTEER　　**MAGICIAN**

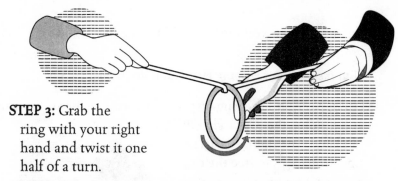

STEP 3: Grab the ring with your right hand and twist it one half of a turn.

"I'm going to tell you a story. Once upon a time, there was a happy little ring, who got himself tangled in some weeds."

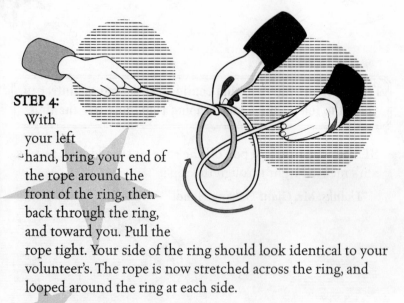

STEP 4: With your left hand, bring your end of the rope around the front of the ring, then back through the ring, and toward you. Pull the rope tight. Your side of the ring should look identical to your volunteer's. The rope is now stretched across the ring, and looped around the ring at each side.

"He twisted and turned himself around and around."

STEP 5: Whew! Pause for a breath, and double-check your work. It should look just like the picture below.

"But he was trapped."

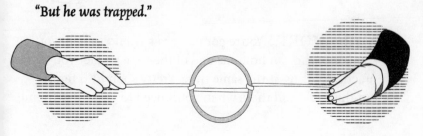

STEP 6: With your right hand, grab the ring from the top, and hold it between your thumb and index finger. With a glance,

make sure your volunteer is holding her end of the rope just as tight as you are!

"But then a Giant Helping Hand came down from the sky..."

STEP 7: Now pull the ring up toward the ceiling. Be sure you're still holding the rope tight with your left hand. The tightness helps undo the loops to free the ring.

"...and freed the little ring!"

> **Trick Tip:** If you're feeling confident, ask your volunteer to play the role of the Giant Helping Hand and free the ring.

STEP 8: The ring will pop off the rope—it should look just like it's melting right through the rope!

"Thanks, Mr. Giant Helping Hand!"

HomeWork: You're gonna need a friend to help you— someone who can hold his end of the rope and let you practice pulling at the same time. Pretty soon he'll figure out the trick, and that's when you'll need to get a new friend!

HaNDY HaNDCuffs #7

assigNment: Remove a ring from a rope that's tied between your two hands!

HaNDs free!
This is pretty sneaky and the audience doesn't even know it. The slip knots in the rope are slippery, so the ring can pass right under them and off your wrist. Beautiful!

from your escapes kit: The rope, large ring

Homemade magic: One handkerchief

Backstage
Less is more and this trick has the least amount of prep of any trick—except for all the other tricks with *no* prep.

sHow time!
"I already know what you're thinking."

STEP 1: Tie one slip knot in one end of the rope. Tie a second slip knot in the other end of the rope. (Check out page 4 if how to do a slip knot has slipped your mind.)

"You're thinking that I'm going to do some kind of a rope trick."

STEP 2: Thread the rope through the ring so that the ring is between the two slip knots.

"And it's a rope trick that involves this metal ring."

STEP 3: Put one slip knot over your right hand at the wrist. Put the other slip knot over your left hand at the wrist. Tighten up both slip knots—not so tight that you get a rope burn, though!

"But this is slightly different. I'm going to get this ring off the rope without untying the knots."

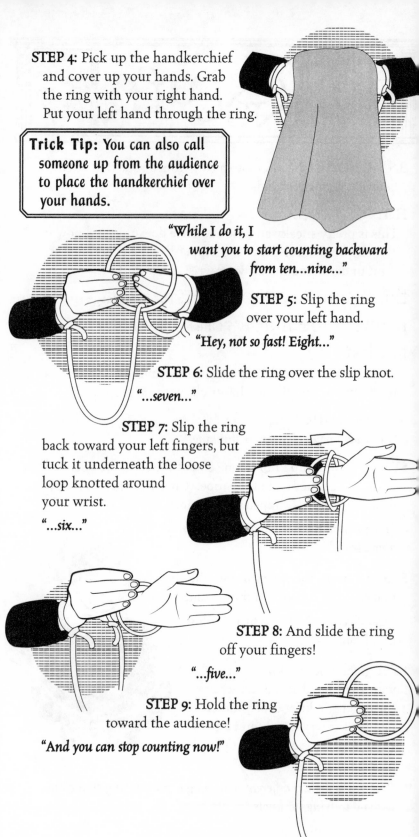

STEP 4: Pick up the handkerchief and cover up your hands. Grab the ring with your right hand. Put your left hand through the ring.

Trick Tip: You can also call someone up from the audience to place the handkerchief over your hands.

"While I do it, I want you to start counting backward from ten...nine..."

STEP 5: Slip the ring over your left hand.

"Hey, not so fast! Eight..."

STEP 6: Slide the ring over the slip knot.

"...seven..."

STEP 7: Slip the ring back toward your left fingers, but tuck it underneath the loose loop knotted around your wrist.

"...six..."

STEP 8: And slide the ring off your fingers!

"...five..."

STEP 9: Hold the ring toward the audience!

"And you can stop counting now!"

homework

No one likes magicians who stare at their hands while they work. That's why they invented mirrors. Stand in front of a mirror and practice sliding the ring off without looking. Also work on keeping your hands as steady as possible—the more you fidget, the more your audience will suspect that something's not right.

now try it this way

You can also reverse the steps and put the ring *onto* the rope. This might be more interesting, since the audience has no idea what you're going to do when you start.

the Knotty Professor

#8

assignment: Remove a metal ring from a rope without untying it!

through and through

Looping can be a lot of fun, and that's what you're doing here. By looping and looping and looping your rope, you're giving the audience the impression that a ring threaded through the rope is getting all twisted up in the rope and becoming more and more difficult to untangle. Fooled 'em! It only looks that way—you're really untying the ring!

magic must-haves: Magic trunk

from your escapes kit:

The large ring, rope

backstage

This is so easy! Just keep your ring clean and your rope soft. Then place both on the magic trunk.

show time!

"It doesn't matter if you have perfect vision, or wear contacts or glasses. Your eyes can trick you. For example, am I putting the rope through the ring..."

STEP 1: Holding the ring in your left hand and the rope in your right hand, thread the rope through the ring so that the rope comes through the "bottom" of the ring and out the "top."

"...or the ring through the rope?"

MAGICIAN'S VIEW

STEP 2: Holding the rope between your right thumb and index finger, bring your right hand down so that it's beside the ring. Move your right pinky in front of the rope and

*   * 32

grab the rope between your pinky and ring finger. Then move your middle finger in front of the rope, so that the rope is looped around your ring finger. Curl your ring finger to hold the loop inside.

"Now, let me ask a similar but different question. Watch the ring..."

STEP 3: With your left hand, rotate the ring a half of a turn (turning it away from your-self). Then push your right hand through the ring, towards yourself, holding the rope tightly.

"Am I putting the ring through my hand..."

STEP 4: Let go of the ring with your left hand. The ring will rest on your wrist like a bracelet.

"...or am I putting my hand through the ring?"

STEP 5: With your left hand, lift the lower end of the rope and hold it near the ring. At this point, the audience simply sees a rope threaded through a ring, but we know there's something tricky happening here. Your right hand hides the audience's view of the extra "looping" of the rope in and out of the ring.

"Look at it another way. Which end of the rope is the end of the rope, and which is the beginning? If the end that was on the bottom is now on the top...is the top now the bottom?"

STEP 6: Then, using both hands, tie a knot with the ends of the rope. Your right hand is pretty busy during this step, because your right ring finger also has to stay curled around the loop in the rope.

"If I tie a knot, is the knot a knot?"

STEP 7: Hold the ring steady with your right hand and pull the knot to your left with your left hand. Keep pulling until the rope is stretched out and the knot is as far as it can be from the ring. The rope will run through your right hand as you pull the knot away. Just make sure to keep the ring steady, and remember, your right ring finger is curled and holds the loop of the rope, creating the illusion that the rope is tied around the ring.

"Or is it not a knot?"

STEP 8: Let go of the knot with your left hand. Then lift the rope and drape both strands over your right index finger.

"See how much fun knot puns can be? Or maybe not."

STEP 9: Now transfer the rope and the ring from your right hand to your left hand. Do this by sliding your left index finger under the rope, so that it takes the place of your right index finger. Then use the fingers of your left hand to grab the loop from around your right ring finger. Tuck the loop behind the ring and hold them both with your left thumb. The rest of the rope should be draped over your left index finger.

"Let's find out right now if the knot is a knot."

STEP 10: With your right hand, take one of the strands that is draped over your left index finger and bring it around the ring (to the right), so that it hangs between you and the ring.

"Watch carefully. Only your eyes can decide for sure."

STEP 11: Again using your right hand, reach through the ring from the front (so you're reaching toward yourself) and grab both strands. Pull them through the ring, away from yourself.

"We'll let it hang for a moment while you decide."

STEP 12: Now let go of everything with your left hand. The ring will drop and catch on the rope! Now your audience is convinced that the rope is really looped through the ring.

"Okay, now here's the part that's going to bother you all night long."

STEP 13: Transfer the rope to your left hand again. Hold the rope so that the ring hangs just below your pinky and the two strands drape over your left index finger. With your right hand, grab the strand that's not going through the ring. Let's call this one strand A. We'll call the other strand (the one that goes through the ring) strand B.

"If I tell you to watch the rope, then you'll probably watch the ring."

STEP 14: Bring strand A back behind and to the left of strand B. Wrap strand A around the last three fingers of your left hand, tucking it between your index finger and your middle finger.

"And if I tell you to watch the ring, then you'll probably watch the rope."

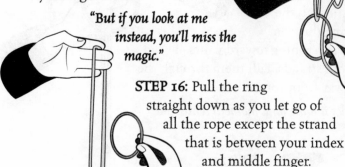

STEP 15: Hold the ring with your right hand.

"But if you look at me instead, you'll miss the magic."

STEP 16: Pull the ring straight down as you let go of all the rope except the strand that is between your index and middle finger.

"Because a moment is all the time I need..."

STEP 17: And the ring will "melt" through the rope!

"...to make the ring escape from the rope!"

HOMEWORK: This is the most complex trick at Magic U. this month because of the many individual steps. But with practice, you'll get it! Try it in front of a mirror to be sure that the loop of rope around your ring finger is hidden from the audience.

Trick Tip: You can make up your own little story to go with this trick. Try a little rabbit running through the woods, a lab rat caught in a maze at the science lab, or a giant bee that can't fly straight. The possibilities are endless!

---

tHe ROPe BURN! #9

assignment: Escape after being tied up with rope!

tie ONe ON!

You're tied up with rope...or are you? You can do things with loops of rope that you can't do when the rope isn't looped. Loops of rope, when tied around or through something like a sleeve, a ring, or a bead, are not tied as securely as they appear—and that's what happens here!

Homemaðe magic: About 50 feet of rope, a jacket or coat with loose sleeves, and a handy closet or screen

extras: A volunteer who doesn't know the trick

> **Trick Tip:** If you don't have a closet handy, you can always use a large cardboard box or a folding screen that you can hide behind.

Backstage

As a good magic student, you probably have a nice coil of rope already lying around the house. And you know that the secret to a good rope trick is to make sure that the rope is nice and soft, right? Wash it in the washing machine and dry it in the dryer until the rope is as soft as your favorite pillow.

Once you have the rope the way you need it, slip on your jacket and get ready for some ropin'!

SHOW time!

"Here's some easy magic math: One rope plus one magician equals what? That's right: A rope trick."

STEP 1: Fold the rope in half at the center so it's now 25 feet long. Hold the two ends in your right hand and the looped bottom in your left hand.

"This is one of the most difficult rope escapes in the world. For you. For me? Not so difficult!"

STEP 2: Now that the rope is doubled over, wrap it around your waist.

Then, thread the two ends through the loop.

"Most escape artists let someone from the audience tie them up, but they won't let that person hold on to the rope during the escape. I'm going to do both. I need a volunteer."

STEP 3: Have your volunteer grab the two ends of the rope, and pull them tight around your waist.

"Don't pull it too tight—I still have to breathe!"

STEP 4: Next, have your volunteer take the two ends of the rope, put them inside your jacket or coat, and down your right jacket or coat sleeve, starting from the shoulder, until the ends appear at your right wrist. This will be awkward and difficult, so make it funny.

"Hey, that tickles! Please don't tickle the magician! No fair tickling!"

STEP 5: Next, get your volunteer to reach up into your sleeve and pull the ends of the rope out of the end of your sleeve.

"I hope you don't put your jacket or coat on this way at home! Your parents would totally freak."

STEP 6: Tell your volunteer to hold on tightly to the two ends of the rope.

"Got a grip? Good, now pull it tight. Everybody close your eyes and I'm going to escape like magic."

STEP 7: Stop for a second, like you just thought of something important.

"You know what? That probably won't work out. Some of you will want to peek. So I need a door..."

STEP 8: Now, walk behind the door. But here's the catch: Bring as much of the rope with you as possible. You're gonna need it.

"...but my volunteer's still going to keep holding on to the rope for me."

STEP 9: Close the door behind you. This will give you enough slack in the rope and it'll prevent your audience from seeing how you escape from the rope. But before you do anything, you gotta impress your audience. Here's what you shout through the door:

"I'm gonna do this in less than ten seconds..."

Trick Tip: Is it hard to find a door around the house? Can't find a place to hide behind or in? Don't sweat it. Try these alternatives: (1) you can hide behind floor-length window curtains; or (2) set up a screen made from large cardboard boxes.

STEP 10: You can get out of the rope in far less time than ten seconds, but this gives the audience something to do and the time limit astounds them! Grab the center of the rope around your waist and pull the loop out using the slack in the rope.

"So, keep your eyes closed, and count out loud to ten."

STEP 11: Push the loop down your right sleeve starting at your shoulder. Work it toward your fingertips. Don't worry about the other rope already in your sleeve.

"Okay, everyone count with me."

STEP 12: Pull the loop out of your right sleeve, near your wrist.

"Ready?"

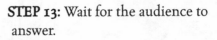

STEP 13: Wait for the audience to answer.

"Start counting. One...two..."

STEP 14: Here's the tricky part. Make the loop as large as you can. That's why you needed to get all that slack in the rope earlier. Pull on the loop to make it bigger.

"...three...four..."

STEP 15: Loop the loop over your head, and lower it down your body. Step over the loop.

"...five..."

STEP 16: Now, you're ready for the last step. Pull all of the rope loop back down and out of your right sleeve. It will be free from your waist.

"...six...seven...eight..."

STEP 17: Hold the rope by the center, and step back through the door. You're free of the rope, and your volunteer is still holding both ends! Ask her to hold the rope out to the audience so they can see it hasn't been cut.

HOMEWORK: If you can't loop, you're going to be stuck behind that door for much longer than ten seconds! Practice creating the loop and stepping through it. Believe it or not, this is the key to the whole trick. You need enough slack to pull the loop away from your waist and toss it over your head and down your body.

ROPE JOKES

Everybody loves a good rope joke, and you can always misdirect an audience better if you keep them laughing, or at least smiling. Here are some great comedy bits you can work on for your act.

"I'd like to do the great rope escape trick for you now, but I'm a little tied up..."

"Hey, don't pull so hard or you'll find out what I had for breakfast!"

And you can probably think of a few puns using "knot" and "not," too.

CHAiR fRee! #10

assignment: Escape from a rope while sitting in a chair!

Rope-a-dope

Escaping from a chair is easy when you're not really tied to it. Because you've positioned the rope in a certain way, it only *looks* like you're tied to the chair.

from your escapes kit: The rope

Homemade magic: One chair (one that's good for tying you to), a handkerchief, a quarter, and a shirt with a pocket

> **Trick Tip:** If you don't have a handkerchief, you can use a bandanna, a scarf, or even a small towel—anything that's big enough to cover up both your hands.

extras: A volunteer who doesn't know the trick

Backstage

Check out the chair for comfort. You don't want to be tied to an uncomfortable chair. And then take the quarter and put it in your shirt pocket.

SHOW time!

"The trick to doing magic with a chair is that you have to find one that's really comfortable."

STEP 1: Sit down on the chair. Wiggle your bottom until it's really comfy.

"This one will do. It fits perfectly."

STEP 2: Choose a volunteer from the audience. Put your knees together, and lay the rope across the tops of your thighs. It should hang evenly over your legs.

"Do you know the secret of escaping from being tied to a chair?"

STEP 3: Bring the ends of the rope together under your knees and separate your knees by about four inches or so.

"Me neither."

STEP 4: Reach through your legs, and pull up both rope ends. Bring your knees back together again.

"But I'm going to try it anyway."

STEP 5: Lay the ends of the rope across your thighs—the right end should lie across your right thigh and the left end should lie across your left. Interlock the fingers of your hands and place them in your lap, over the top of the rope.

"I'll need some help, though."

STEP 6: Pick a volunteer and ask him to tie the rope around your wrists as tightly as possible. But not so tight that it hurts. Magic should only be painful to your volunteers!

If your volunteer can't tie a knot, fire him and order up a new volunteer. Or, you could teach him how to knot. *You* know how, thanks to pages 3 and 4.

"Here, tie my hands and legs together with this rope."

STEP 7: After your volunteer ties you up, you'll instantly see the solution. You can escape whenever you want. But we're going to make it more interesting.

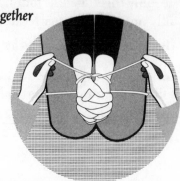

"Now, take this handkerchief and place it on my lap."

STEP 8: Make sure the handkerchief covers up your hands.

"If I can't escape from a chair, and I'm stuck here, it won't be so bad, really. I'll just sit and watch TV."

STEP 9: Here's how to get out of the rope: Just separate your knees a little bit and the rope will provide enough slack so you can remove one or both hands instantly. Let's just get one hand out first, though, and have some fun with the audience.

"But if that gets boring, maybe I could just read a book."

STEP 10: Slip your left hand from the rope, take it out from under the handkerchief, and hold it out like you want someone to hand you something.

"Does anyone have an interesting book I could read?"

STEP 11: Now, put your left hand back under the handkerchief, and back inside the rope. Put your knees together. Turn to your volunteer.

"Whoa! What was that all about? You better remove the handkerchief and see what's going on."

STEP 12: Your volunteer lifts the handkerchief, but your hands are back in place, still "tightly tied." Pretty cool, huh?

"You better put the handkerchief back. I'll try this again."

STEP 13: Once the handkerchief is back in place, repeat step 10, only this time use your right hand, perhaps removing a silly prop like the quarter from your pocket.

"But if I sit in a chair for too long, I get hungry. Here's a quarter."

STEP 14: Toss the quarter to the audience. The audience will be following the quarter through the air.

"Could someone go down to the store and buy me some candy?"

STEP 15: Put your right hand back under the scarf. Now push the rope down your knees to your feet and kick it up in the air to make your final escape.

"Oh, wait. I'll just go get some myself!"

HOMEWORK: The trick here is being able to create enough slack so that your hands can slip out easily. Grab a friend (who won't be your volunteer from the audience) and let him practice tying you to the chair.

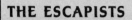

THE ESCAPISTS

Magicians who specialize in escape tricks are more formally known as *escapologists*. They've become such good friends with pieces of rope that they can escape while tied up standing, sitting, lying down, you name it. Sometimes, instead of rope, they'll use chains (as you know from experience!) or handcuffs.

Some magicians have even escaped from tape! Irv Weiner (1923-1999), a famous magician from Boston known as "Mr. Fingers," used to have an audience member tie his thumbs together with red tape, from which he'd free himself. (Wouldn't you know it? The method's called a Thumb Tie.)

Breakfast of Champions! #11

assignment: Remove breakfast cereal from a string without breaking any!

Breaking eggs

You can't make an omelet without breaking some eggs, and you can't do this trick without breaking a Cheerio®. Fortunately, the audience doesn't realize that you're breaking the popular breakfast food.

magic must-haves: Magic trunk

Homemade magic: One handkerchief or napkin, one 12-inch piece of thin string, and a box of Cheerios

> **Trick Tip:** Did your little brother or sister eat all the Cheerios? Don't worry. This trick will work with any cereal that has a hole in the center (for example, Froot Loops).

extras: Two volunteers who totally don't know the trick

Backstage

Here's magic rule #1: *Don't* eat the props. Save enough Cheerios for the trick! Set the box of Cheerios, the string, and the handkerchief on the magic trunk.

Show time!

"Welcome to Breakfast Cereal Theater! I'm going to tell you a little story. The story of Robin Hood."

STEP 1: Hold out your string and hand it to someone in the audience to check out.

"Here is my stage. Check it out and you'll see it's just a regular piece of string."

STEP 2: Take the box of Cheerios and hand it to someone else in the audience.

"And here is a whole box of tasty actors. Open it up for me and let's get started!"

STEP 3: Take back the string and hold it in one hand. Reach into the box of Cheerios. Yell, **"Ow! It's got me! It's got me!"** Then laugh, pull out one Cheerio, and say, **"False alarm."** Thread the Cheerio on the string.

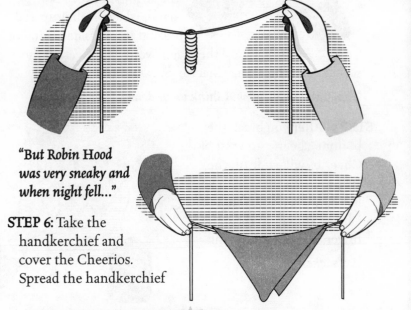

"Once upon a time, Robin Hood and his band of Merry Men were caught by the Sheriff of Nottingham."

STEP 4: Bring the ends of the string together evenly, so that the one Cheerio hangs at the bottom. Thread at least eight or nine more Cheerios through the string; but this time make sure that both ends of the string go through the holes. Check out the picture to see what we mean.

"One by one, the Sheriff tied them all together. They were trapped! None of them could escape! And just to be sure, the Sheriff had two giant guards watching over them."

STEP 5: Give each end of the string to a volunteer (that means you need two). Have them stand far away from one another, so that the string is stretched almost horizontal.

"But Robin Hood was very sneaky and when night fell..."

STEP 6: Take the handkerchief and cover the Cheerios. Spread the handkerchief along the string to provide enough cover to hide your two hands when you place them underneath.

"...the most amazing thing happened."

STEP 7: Now, reach under the handkerchief with your two hands.

"Robin got himself some magic help! He knew a magician who could help him. All Robin needed was some friends to say the magic words: 'Sherwood Forest.'"

STEP 8: Tell the audience to yell out *"Sherwood Forest"* when you give the signal. As they yell it, grasp the bottom Cheerio (that very first one you put on the string) between both hands, shake it slightly, and break it in two. The yelling of the magic word will cover up the sound of the breaking Cheerio. Sneaky, huh?

"Congratulations, gang. I think we've done it."

STEP 9: After you break the bottom Cheerio, the rest of the Cheerios will slide off the string. Catch them with your left hand. Hold the broken Cheerio pieces in the curled fingers of your right hand.

"Let's take a look."

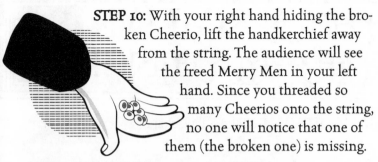

STEP 10: With your right hand hiding the broken Cheerio, lift the handkerchief away from the string. The audience will see the freed Merry Men in your left hand. Since you threaded so many Cheerios onto the string, no one will notice that one of them (the broken one) is missing.

"Robin Hood and his Merry Men are free!"

STEP 11: Place the handkerchief back in your pocket along with the broken Cheerio. This is a technique the magicians call, *Going South with the Evidence.* The audience is only watching your left hand, so your right hand is free to hide the Cheerio.

"The guards were reassigned to clean the horse stables and Robin Hood and his Merry Men returned to Sherwood Forest, just in time for breakfast."

STEP 12: Take the Cheerios from your left hand and pop them into your mouth.

"My breakfast."

HOMEWORK: Timing is everything in a trick like this. Your cue to break the Cheerio comes exactly as the audience yells out the magic words "Sherwood Forest." You have to do it just right so no one actually hears the snap. (Also, you should practice catching the broken Cheerio—you don't want to drop it on the floor and give away your secret!)

tHAt's ReaLLy tHuMB-tHiNG! #12

assignment: Take off a jacket or coat when your thumbs are tied together!

sLack attack

Slack is a great thing with rope and string tricks. By creating slack in the string—making it not as tight as it appears—makes it easy, oh so easy, to slip out of it.

Homemade magic: One piece of string, the stiffer, the better; and a jacket or coat

> **Trick Tip:** What? You don't have any string? Try a pipe cleaner or a shoelace.

extras: One volunteer from the audience who doesn't know the trick

Backstage

Take to the stage with only one thing on your mind: Slack!

Show time!

"This is a magic trick that goes all the way back to the great Pinetti in the late 1700s. (Never heard of him? That's okay. Just remember: Pinetti. Rhymes with spaghetti.)"

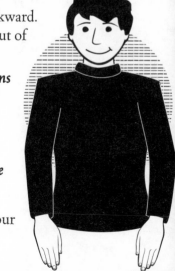

STEP 1: Slip a jacket or coat on backward. Don't zip it up—we can't get you out of that one without scissors!

"Anyway, this is a trick that magicians have used for more than 250 years..."

STEP 2: Show your string to the audience.

"... probably since the invention of the jacket."

STEP 3: Hold the string between your thumbs and index fingers. Your

★ ★ 56

hands should be about two inches apart with the palms facing each other.

"Now, I need a volunteer."

STEP 4: Call up a volunteer from the audience.

"I want you to tie my thumbs together. You don't know how the great Pinetti used to tie himself up, so I'll talk you through it and the audience can watch."

MAGICIAN'S VIEW

STEP 5: Now, fold your hands together—with the fingers interlocking. But do it in a special way. Keep your right middle finger bent inside your hands. As you clasp your hands together, the right middle finger presses down the center on the string—creating slack or a loop in the string. Do this quickly, so no one can see it happen.

"When my thumbs are tied together, my arms and body become a circle so solid that nothing can penetrate it—or so it will seem. Now grab the ends and tie them around my thumbs. Make an overhand knot."

STEP 6: Watch carefully as your volunteer does the job. If she doesn't know what an overhead knot is, clue her in, using your know-how from page 3. Once that knot is done, she's got to tie another.

"Now, tie another knot over those same thumbs."

STEP 7: This time, cross your thumbs, right over left, before she ties the knot. Don't worry, no one will notice that your right middle finger is still hiding inside your palm. The thumbs hide everything!

"Nice and tight. There! See how my thumbs are already turning purple?"

Congratulations! You've just mastered the *Thumb Tie.* Anytime you want, you can slip one of your thumbs out by simply releasing the hidden loop of string that's held down by your right middle finger. When you replace your thumb in the thumb tie, press your right middle finger back on the string. The slack goes away, and the knots seem tight again!

STEP 8: As you face the audience, turn your body to your left. Lower your arms, so the jacket or coat slides off your shoulders and down your arms.

"Well, I'm in here pretty tight. I wonder if I can do this."

STEP 9: When the jacket or coat is covering your hands, secretly slip your left hand (the one farthest away from the audience) out of the thumb tie. The jacket or coat will slide down your arms toward the floor.

"Jackets are pretty tricky..."

STEP 10: The sleeves will begin to turn inside out. Pull your left hand out first, and then your right hand. Without dropping the jacket or coat on the floor (especially if it's not your jacket or coat), sneak your left thumb back into the knot.

"...but magicians are trickier."

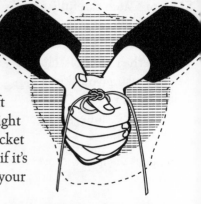

VIEW UNDER JACKET

STEP 11: Your jacket or coat is off. You've escaped from your jacket or coat, and the knot is still a knot! Let your volunteer inspect the knots to be sure they are still tied.

"Now, who wants to cut me out of here? Carefully?"

HOMEWORK:
If you can't do the thumb tie, you're not going to slip out of the jacket or coat. Find a friend who can tie you up—we all have a friend like that—and practice creating the slack so that you can slip your hand out and back in again.

NOW TRY IT THIS WAY
Have a volunteer hold the top of a broomstick and pass your tied thumbs "through it" by secretly slipping your thumb in and out of the knot as you move your hands closer to him.

EXTRA CREDIT
Find some small hula hoops or rings (but nothing heavy enough to knock you out). Have a volunteer toss them at you. Instead of catching them in your hands, quickly slip out of the thumb tie and catch them on one of your arms. The rings have penetrated your arm, like magic!

SUPER EXTRA CREDIT!
Let's call this one a Chair Tie. Once you're thumb tied, find a chair that has spindles or rungs on its back. As you pick up the chair, slip out of the tie, put your hands around the rungs, and slip back into the tie. It'll look like your hands have become tied to the chair! Act surprised!

ALL THUMBS!

The *Thumb Tie* was probably invented in Asia but there is evidence that Europeans performed this trick in public first.

But the first performer to make his reputation on this baffling knot trick was the Japanese magician Ten Ichi, who performed it about a hundred years ago. Twentieth-century magicians who used the Thumb Tie routine included DeBier, Carl Rosini, Jean Hugard, and Harry Willard. Today, Mac King and Jonathan Neal do the thumb tie and many variations of it as part of their show.

assignment: Free a quarter from a paper jail!

know when to fold it

Folding paper is an ancient art that every magician needs to learn. When you fold paper in a certain way, the folds around your quarter are designed to let it slip out secretly into your hand.

homemade magic: One quarter and one 5-inch-square piece of paper

extras: Two volunteers who don't know the trick

backstage

Relax—there's no prep work to do. Just get up in front of the audience and start making the magic!

show time!

"Money is very tricky."

STEP 1: Hold up the quarter with your left hand and place it on the square piece of paper—just above the center. Press the quarter against the paper with your thumb to keep it in place.

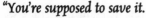

*"You're supposed to save it.
'Put some away for a rainy day,' my dad always says."*

MAGICIAN'S VIEW

STEP 2: Fold the bottom edge of the paper up to within 1/2 inch of the top. Keep the quarter where it is. To make this trick even better, keep pressing the quarter

against the paper so that it makes an impression. This'll
help fool the audience once you've slipped the quarter out.

"But that never works for me."

STEP 3: Fold the right side
of the paper to the back.

*"Whenever I get extra
money..."*

STEP 4: Fold
the left side of
the paper to
the back.

*"...I take my dad's advice and
try to save it."*

**SECRET
OPENING**

STEP 5: Fold the top—in this
case, the top is the little half-
inch strip—down over the
back. Now, thanks to all the
folding, the quarter looks like it's
all wrapped up tight. But only you
know there's a "secret opening" at the
top edge.

"I make a nice hiding place."

**SECRET
OPENING**

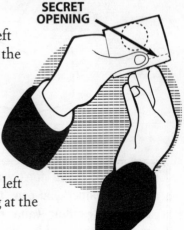

STEP 6: Pass the paper from your left
hand to your right hand, turning the
folded paper upside down so the
secret opening is on the bottom.
The quarter that was on the
bottom is now at the top.

"And it seems very strong."

STEP 7: Put the paper back in your left
hand, keeping the secret opening at the
bottom.

"Very safe and very secure."

STEP 8: Pick a volunteer and say to him,

"Can you feel the coin? It's there, right?"

STEP 9: Let him feel the quarter, while you keep squeezing the paper below it so it doesn't move. Then pick a new volunteer to feel the quarter, asking her,

"How about you? Can you feel the coin, too?"

STEP 10: After both volunteers have felt the coin, bring your right hand up to the paper. Relax your left thumb and let the quarter secretly slide into your right palm.

"So it's safe, right?"

STEP 11: Turn to your first volunteer again. Transfer the folded paper from your right hand back to your left.

"And you're sure you felt it in there?"

STEP 12: They'll nod or say, "yes." As they do this, slip your right hand—very casually—down into your pocket and drop the quarter in there.

"That's funny, because if I get some magic lint from my pocket..."

STEP 13: Bring up your right hand and pretend you're sprinkling something over the paper.

"...and sprinkle it over the paper..."

Trick Tip: If you don't want to sprinkle "magic pocket lint" over the paper, you can "tap" the coin through the paper using your magic wand, flick the paper with your right middle finger, or blow on it. Whatever works for you!

"...my quarter disappears!"

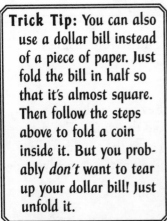

Trick Tip: You can also use a dollar bill instead of a piece of paper. Just fold the bill in half so that it's almost square. Then follow the steps above to fold a coin inside it. But you probably *don't* want to tear up your dollar bill! Just unfold it.

HOMEWORK: This isn't origami—the Japanese art of paper folding—but it's close. This trick depends on your ability to fold paper the right way and in the right order. Practice until you can fold the paper without looking at it—use a mirror if you need to.

NOW try it this way

As you know by now, the way to improve your act is to develop and change your patter so that it sounds more like you. For example, here's a patter tip for this trick: Create a story about George Washington (the coin) being surrounded on all sides by the enemy (the paper) and miraculously escaping.

free the BiRD! #14

assignment: Make a coin vanish from inside a handkerchief!

wrap it up!

Wrist, handkerchief, and coins—they go together like toppings on a pizza. When you hold the coin under the handkerchief and turn your hand over, the coin actually ends up outside the handkerchief before the coin is wrapped.

magic must-haves: Magic trunk

Homemade magic: One coin with the American

bald eagle on the back—like a half-dollar or a silver dollar, and one handkerchief or bandanna that you can't see through

Backstage

Place the coin and the handkerchief side by side on the magic trunk. It doesn't get any easier than that!

show time!

"You know what my favorite bird is?"

STEP 1: With the coin in your left hand, show both sides of it to the audience so they can see the eagle on the back.

"Right, it's the American bald eagle. They have a wingspan of more than six feet."

STEP 2: Spread your arms apart as far as you can.

"They're really big birds."

STEP 3: Hold up the handkerchief to the audience. You should now have the coin in your left hand and the hanky in your right. (If the coin sneezes, just wipe its nose with the handkerchief and keep going.)

"And that makes them hard to catch."

STEP 4: Hold the coin in your left hand, palm up. The coin should be between your thumb and your fingers. Place the handkerchief over the coin and your left hand.

"In fact, they're so difficult to capture, we have to use special handkerchiefs."

STEP 5: With your right hand, lift the coin from your left hand, but just a little bit. The handkerchief should fall over the coin. Keep your left hand underneath the handkerchief.

"Now the bald eagle is ours!"

STEP 6: Stick the coin back in your left fingertips. Here's the tricky part. As you're placing the coin, your left thumb should be pressing a piece of the handkerchief against the back of the coin. Don't let the audience see this happen!

"Or is it?"

STEP 7: Lift the front of the handkerchief up and over the coin to show the coin to the audience. You'll still have a piece of the handkerchief pressed against the back of the coin with your left thumb. Then cover up the coin again.

"Unlike some animals, bald eagles don't do well in captivity."

STEP 8: This next move is simple, but you gotta do it just right. You're just turning your left hand over—but you're doing it in a very special way.

Right now, your left thumb is away from your audience and pointing up. Now, bend your left wrist down. Your left thumb will be toward the audience and pointing down. Pull the part of the handkerchief that's on your wrist forward, so that it hangs over the quarter.

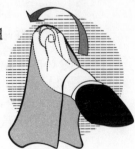

The coin should now be on the outside of the handkerchief on the side facing you (and still covered by the handkerchief on the other side).

"They need a lot of fresh air and sunshine."

STEP 9: With your right hand, twist the handkerchief below the coin so that its shape can be seen through the material. The edge of the folded handkerchief should curl over the top of the coin.

Trick Tip: Shake your left hand a little bit to get the handkerchief to completely drape down, or use your right hand to do it for you!

"They're also really squirmy. They twist and turn, and peck at you with their beaks."

STEP 10: To the audience, the coin seems to be trapped inside the handkerchief. Show this to the audience.

"And they let you know that no cage or handkerchief is ever going to hold them."

STEP 11: Now it's the big payoff! Very slowly, pull the coin up and make it look like it's coming through the handkerchief—as if there's a hole or slit in the handkerchief.

"They find a secret way out...and... whammo! They're gone."

STEP 12: At the end, place the coin down and open the handkerchief to show the audience that there is no hole.

"Free as a bird!"

HOMEWORK: The wrist move in Step 8 is essential to the trick's success. You have to be able to flip your wrist while keeping the exposed side of the quarter hidden. Practice in front of a mirror until you can do it just right.

assignment: Make a Life Saver candy escape from a piece of string!

save a Life (saver)

This trick works because you have *two* Life Savers, but the audience thinks you only have one. With some tricky sleight of hand, you're going to replace a gimmicked Life Saver with a normal one.

Homemade magic: One 3-foot piece of string, two white Life Savers, a handkerchief, white glue, a jacket with pockets

extras: A volunteer from the audience and a grown-up

Trick Tip: Allergic to Life Savers? No problem! This trick works with all kinds of great food: small pretzels, Cheerios, Froot Loops, anything you can thread on a string and easily break.

Backstage

Find an adult to help you create this gimmick. Ask him or her to break one of the Life Savers into two equal pieces. (He or she can use scissors or a sharp knife, or his or her bare hands if he or she's strong enough.) Glue the two halves back together. You can probably handle the gluing part.

In your right-hand pocket, place the other (unbroken) Life Saver and the handkerchief.

sHow time!

"Did you know that Life Savers sometimes get into trouble?"

STEP 1: Show the gimmicked Life Saver and the piece of string.

"That's right. Sometimes they need to have their own lives saved."

STEP 2: Thread the string through the hole in the gimmicked Life Saver.

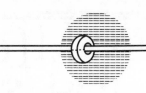

"See? He's done it again!"

STEP 3: Tie a square knot in the string, about 4 inches above the gimmicked Life Saver. (Are you square on square knots? Check out pages 3–4 if not.)

"He's gotten into some kind of jam! But don't worry, I can save him. But I'm going to need some help."

STEP 4: Call up a volunteer from the audience and hand her the ends of the string.

"Hold this tight! Whatever you do, don't let go!"

STEP 5: As she takes the string, reach into your right pocket, and remove the handkerchief, secretly bringing along the normal Life Saver, too. (Don't let anyone see the normal Life Saver.)

"Our Life Saver is depending on us!"

STEP 6: Put the handkerchief over the gimmicked Life Saver and the string.

The gimmicked Life Saver should be completely covered.

"The first thing we have to do is make it dark. Life Savers love the dark—it keeps them from panicking."

STEP 7: Here's the fun part: Reach under the scarf with both hands. Press your ear against the handkerchief and pretend to listen to the Life Saver.

"What's that? You need a magic word?"

STEP 8: Turn to the audience and tell them:

"Everyone, please say the magic words: 'Life Saver, save your life!'"

STEP 9: As the audience says the magic words, snap the gimmicked Life Saver and break it into its two pieces. If the audience is loud enough, they shouldn't hear the Life Saver break. Put both pieces in your left hand.

"I think that did it! I think he's going to be okay!"

STEP 10: Keep the broken Life Saver in your left hand under the scarf. Bring your right hand and the normal Life Saver out from under the scarf as you pull the scarf away with your left hand. The audience will only see the normal Life Saver.

"Look, it worked! He's safe and sound!"

STEP 11: Now hide the evidence. While everyone is looking at your right hand, use your left hand to put the handkerchief and the broken Life Saver in your left pocket.

"It's not easy to save the life of a Life Saver!"

STEP 12: Put the normal Life Saver in your mouth and crunch it up—and throw the glued one in the trash when no one's looking. (Don't eat that one! Ugh!)

HOMEWORK: The switch is everything here, so practice bringing out the normal Life Saver from your pocket and hiding it under the handkerchief. Using a mirror for practice can really help!

Homemade Handcuffs #16

assignment: Escape from handcuffs made from rope!

prisoners of the rope

This is not as tricky as it looks; it's just really cool! By looping the rope over the other person's right hand and then under, you simply pass the rope "through" the person's hand, "unlocking" the 'cuffs.

Homemade magic: Two pieces of rope about 4 or 5 feet long (you can use the rope from your ESCAPES KIT as one of the ropes)

extras: Two volunteers who can't figure out knots

Backstage

Tie two slip knots at both ends of both ropes. (Slip away to page 4 if you don't remember how to tie slip knots.) The loops should be big enough to easily fit over your wrists.

show time!

"Before we start, I need two volunteers from the audience."

STEP 1: Hold up the ropes to show the audience. When the first volunteer appears, take one of the ropes and loop the ends over her wrists and tighten—but not too much!

"Before they invented metal handcuffs, police had to use rope."

STEP 2: Then take the second rope and loop it on the left wrist of your second volunteer. Thread the end of the rope once between your first volunteer's rope and her body. Loop the end to your second volunteer's wrist and tighten it up. Your two volunteers are now locked together!

"These old-fashioned handcuffs worked pretty well. Nobody could escape from them. Go ahead and try."

STEP 3: Let your friends struggle as they try to escape.

"You can try any way you want, but you can't cut the rope or untie your wrists."

STEP 4: They won't be able to figure it out. So when they give up, switch places with one of your volunteers.

"All right. You've had your fun. Let me show you how it's done."

STEP 5: Grab the center of your rope and slip it through the loop that is around the other person's right wrist (let's call it loop 1), pulling your rope toward your volunteer's right hand. You have now created a new loop (let's call it loop 2).

LOOP 2

"There was one guy who could escape from these handcuffs."

STEP 6: Pull loop 2 so that you can stretch it over the fingers of your volunteer's right hand.

"He was a magician."

STEP 7: And then pull loop 2 down beneath your volunteer's right hand.

"And he knew how to use the invisible key..."

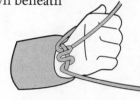

VIEW FROM BELOW

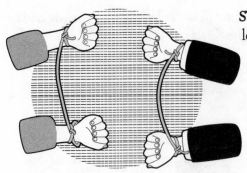

STEP 8: Finally, push loop 2 back through loop 1, and the ropes will unlink. You have "escaped."

"...to free himself."

HOMEWORK:

Making loop 2 is everything here. Find a friend you can practice with and work on steps 5 through 7 together. Once you've mastered these steps, you're ready for an audience!

Trick Tip: Party on! This is a great party game. Next time you're with a group of friends, bring several ropes and have lots of pairs of people tied up at the same time, all trying to escape. They'll never figure out how to do it!

RiNG-a-LiNG #17

assignment: Remove a ring from a knot in a piece of string!

Ring it up

Knots are fun to play with. Through a secret hole in a cup, you secretly untie the knot with your index finger and set the ring free. The audience doesn't see this, of course, and you look like a true magician!

magic must-haves: Magic trunk

Homemade magic: One 18-inch piece of string, one borrowed finger ring, one 12- or 16-ounce plastic, paper, or Styrofoam cup, one pair of scissors or sharp knife

Backstage

This is one of those tricks for which you'll need an adult's help —just with the knife part, though! Have your adult cut a hole in the back of the cup. The hole should be large enough so your index finger can fit through it, and the hole should be about an inch from the bottom of the cup. Drop the string inside the cup and you're good to go!

show time!

"Can I borrow a ring from someone in the audience?"

STEP 1: Pick up the cup and put the string onto the magic trunk.

"Don't worry. No harm will come to it."

STEP 2: Place the cup, mouth down, on the table. Make sure the hole faces you so the audience can't see it. Hold the ring in one hand.

"I promise."

STEP 3: Pick up the string and thread it through the borrowed ring.

"I want to tell you a story about a magician who tried to buy a nice bracelet to give to his wife for her birthday."

STEP 4: Tie an overhand knot in the string, about an inch from the ring. Don't make the knot too tight. (All this talk about an overhand knot over your head? Then look at page 3.)

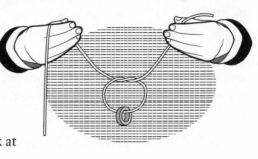

"But the nearest jewelry store only sold rings, not bracelets. So, he bought a ring, and tied it to a piece of magic string."

STEP 5: Let go of the string with your left hand and hold it with your right hand. With your left hand, pick up the cup. Hold the cup only with the tips of your fingers and thumb. Let the end of the string dangle in the cup, but keep the ring and the knot above the cup.

AUDIENCE'S VIEW

"Then he tried a spell to turn the ring into a bracelet."

STEP 6: Swing the string and ring like a pendulum, while telling the audience to watch the knot. At the same time, secretly insert your index finger into the hole in the cup.

"But the magic string thought that the magician's wife would prefer a ring to a bracelet..."

MAGICIAN'S VIEW

STEP 7: Slowly lower the end of the string into the cup until the knot reaches the bottom of the cup and the audience can't see it anymore.

"...so it refused to participate in the spell."

STEP 8: Here's the fun part. Your index finger is inside the cup. Stick your finger through the knot in the string (not the ring).

"It untied itself from the ring..."

STEP 9: Slowly pull the string upward with your right hand. Because your left index finger is sticking through the knot, the knot will begin to untie itself. When the string is pulled completely from the cup, the knot will be untied and the ring will fall into the bottom of the cup.

"...and told the magician to forget about giving his wife a bracelet."

STEP 10: Slip your finger out of the cup and pour the ring onto the magic trunk. Be sure not to let your audience see the hole in the cup!

"The string was right! The wife loved the ring just as it was. I bet you're glad, too, that I didn't magically change your ring!"

HOMEWORK: The hard part here is holding the cup and maneuvering your finger inside. Practice this move in the mirror so that it looks very natural and smooth!

Trick Tip: If you don't have a ring, you can use this same trick to make a knot disappear. Tie a loose knot in the string and lower it into the cup. Stick your hidden finger in the cup and, as you pull the string out, your finger will untie the knot!

LOOP tHE LOOP tHE LOOP #18

assignment: Remove a ring from a loop of string!

tHe Loopy Loop

The reason this trick works so well is because it's an illusion. The ring isn't locked into place at all—it only looks that way. When you manipulate the loop correctly, it looks like you're tying it tighter, but you're really making it looser.

magic must-haves: Magic trunk

from your escapes kit: Small ring

Homemade magic: 6 feet of string

Trick Tip: Tired of working with string? Try a beaded chain (like the kind they use on key chains) or a necklace or a red ribbon. You can use anything that is flexible like string and can be tied in a loop.

---

extras: One volunteer who doesn't know the secret!

Backstage

Tie the ends of the string together to create a loop that's three feet long. Place the loop and the ring on the magic trunk.

sHow time!

"This ring reminds me a lot of the great escape artist Harry Houdini."

STEP 1: Hold up the ring for the audience to see.

"He wasn't round or made of silver, but he could escape from anything: iron shackles, handcuffs, locked jail cells, and yes, even a length of string!"

STEP 2: Thread the loop through the ring. Don't tie it!

"Which is exactly what this ring can do."

STEP 3: Now, hook the loop over your volunteer's thumbs and move the ring to the center of the looped piece of string.

"Sometimes, Harry would tie himself between two posts so that his escape looked even more difficult."

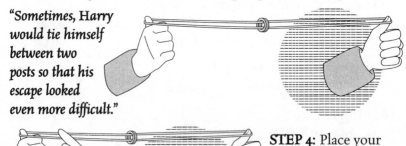

STEP 4: Place your left index finger across both strands between the ring and your volunteer's right thumb.

"But Harry's wife, Bess, would always help him in some way."

STEP 5: Here's a big hint—everything you do from now on in this trick will be done only with the bottom piece of string in the loop. Let's call this piece strand A. With your right thumb and index finger, pinch a section of strand A that's on the left side of the ring.

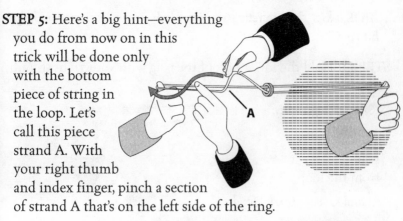

"To the audience, it always looked like she was helping them, not Harry."

STEP 6: Ask your volunteer to give you a little slack in the loop. Then lift the pinched string over your left finger and loop it clockwise around your volunteer's right thumb.

"But she wasn't."

STEP 7: With your right thumb and index finger, let go of the strand. Keep your left index finger in the loop, though.

"It was all part of the illusion."

STEP 8: Now, with your right thumb and first finger, pinch the section of strand A that's between the ring and your volunteer's *left* thumb.

"She was really just making it easier for him to escape."

STEP 9: Lift the section you're now holding over your left index finger, just as you did in step 6. Again, loop it clockwise around your volunteer's right thumb.

A

"Sometimes, she'd kiss him for luck right before his escape. Don't worry—I'm not about to pucker up!"

STEP 10: Let go with your right thumb and first finger.

"In that kiss, she'd secretly pass him a lock pick or special key to help him out."

STEP 11: Hold the lower part of the ring with your right thumb and index finger.

"She was a genius..."

STEP 12: Remove your left finger from the loop.

"...and so was Harry Houdini."

STEP 13: With your right hand, slide the ring to your right side and it will come off as your volunteer's hands separate!

"And so is this ring!"

HOMEWORK:

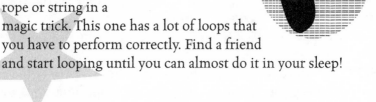

Looping is the fine art of manipulating rope or string in a magic trick. This one has a lot of loops that you have to perform correctly. Find a friend and start looping until you can almost do it in your sleep!

CONCLUSION

Congratulations, you're now an official "Master Escapologist!" You've escaped from Magic U. this month and we couldn't be happier!

We know there were lots of instructions and lots of little steps. Everything had to be done in the correct order or else you would have ended up tied up in knots! And your audience would have been laughing and pointing at you instead of gasping in amazement.

Are you still practicing? Can you tie one of those great fake knots in your sleep? When you see a box of Cheerios do you start looking for a piece of string?

Houdini knew that practice is the only thing that made a magic trick great. That's why he spent so much time practicing with his wife Bess and brother Theo. He could always trust them to keep his secrets. We hope you found a friend or two who could keep yours.

Join us next month for more magic, more tricks, and more tips in the next installment of Magic University!

WHAT'S NEW WITH MAGICIANS JOHN RAILING AND DANNY ORLEANS

Danny Orleans

Once, when Danny was doing a magic show in a school gym, a bee started flying around the room, startling all the kids. But Danny used his magic to take care of it! He picked up a jumbo playing card and swatted it out of the air. The bee landed in a magic box; the box trapped it until after the show, when Danny released the bee outdoors.

John Railing

John likes to think big—right now, he's working on a life-size pop-up book of the solar system. When we say life-size, we mean as big as a person. It would be tough to get a book as big as the solar system into the house!

WHAT'S NEW WITH TOM MASON AND DAN DANKO

Tom Mason

Tom is 90% water, 6% laziness, 2% sugar-coated breakfast cereal, and 2% magic. He'd like to be a larger percentage of magic, but the laziness and the water are too strong to resist.

Dan Danko

Dan is also 90% water and 2% magic; the rest of him is 6% video games, and 2% sushi. He'd like to be a larger percentage of video games.